A LOOK AT US HISTORY

THE AMERICAN REVOLUTION

BY PETER CASTELLANO

Gareth Stevens PUBLISHING

CRASHCOURSE

Please visit our website, www.garethstevens.com. For a free color catalog of all our high-quality books, call toll free 1-800-542-2595 or fax 1-877-542-2596.

Library of Congress Cataloging-in-Publication Data

Names: Castellano, Peter, author.
Title: The American Revolution / Peter Castellano.
Description: New York : Gareth Stevens Publishing, [2018] | Series: A look at US history | Includes bibliographical references and index.
Identifiers: LCCN 2016030415| ISBN 9781482460230 (paperback) | ISBN 9781482460247 (6 pack) | ISBN 9781482460254 (library bound)
Subjects: LCSH: United States--History--Revolution, 1775-1783--Juvenile literature.
Classification: LCC E208 .C36 2018 | DDC 973.3--dc23
LC record available at https://lccn.loc.gov/2016030415

First Edition

Published in 2018 by
Gareth Stevens Publishing
111 East 14th Street, Suite 349
New York, NY 10003

Designer: Samantha DeMartin
Editor: Kristen Nelson

Photo credits: Series art Christophe BOISSON/Shutterstock.com; feather quill Galushko Sergey/Shutterstock.com; parchment mollicart-design/Shutterstock.com; cover, p. 1 DEA PICTURE LIBRARY/De Agostini/Getty Images; pp. 5, 17 UniversalImagesGroup/Universal Images Group/Getty Images; p. 7 Interim Archives/Archive Photos/Getty Images; p. 9 Bettmann/Bettmann/Getty Images; p. 11 Slick-o-bot/Wikimedia Commons; p. 13 MPI/Archive Photos/Getty Images; pp. 15, 23 Everett Historical/Shutterstock.com; p. 19 NYPL/Wikimedia Commons; p. 21 (main) courtesy of the Library of Congress; p. 21 (inset) Stock Montage/Archive Photos/Getty Images; p. 25 DEA/G. DAGLI ORTI/De Agostini Picture Library/Getty Images; p. 27 Ed Vebell/Archive Photos/Getty Images; p. 29 Electric_Crayon/DigistalVision Vectors/Getty Images; p. 30 (timeline) Aleksandr Bryliaev/Shutterstock.com.

Printed in the United States of America

CPSIA compliance information: Batch #CS17GS: For further information contact Gareth Stevens, New York, New York at 1-800-542-2595.

CONTENTS

Words in the glossary appear in **bold** type the first time they are used in the text.

FOR FREEDOM!

Before the American Revolution, the country we know as the United States was 13 **colonies**. The colonists felt their mother country, Great Britain, didn't listen to them. Many colonists wanted to become an independent nation. Some believed war was the only way to win freedom.

MAKE THE GRADE

Colonists fought alongside the British during the French and Indian War, which ended in 1763. Great Britain needed money after this war and looked to the colonies for it.

CAUSES OF THE WAR

For years, the colonists mostly governed themselves with little British control. They considered themselves British citizens. Then, the British started making new laws. The colonists felt they were being suddenly controlled. First, the Proclamation of 1763 stated colonists couldn't settle beyond the Appalachian Mountains.

MAKE THE GRADE

The British practice of allowing the colonies a lot of independence is called salutary neglect. It went on for about 150 years.

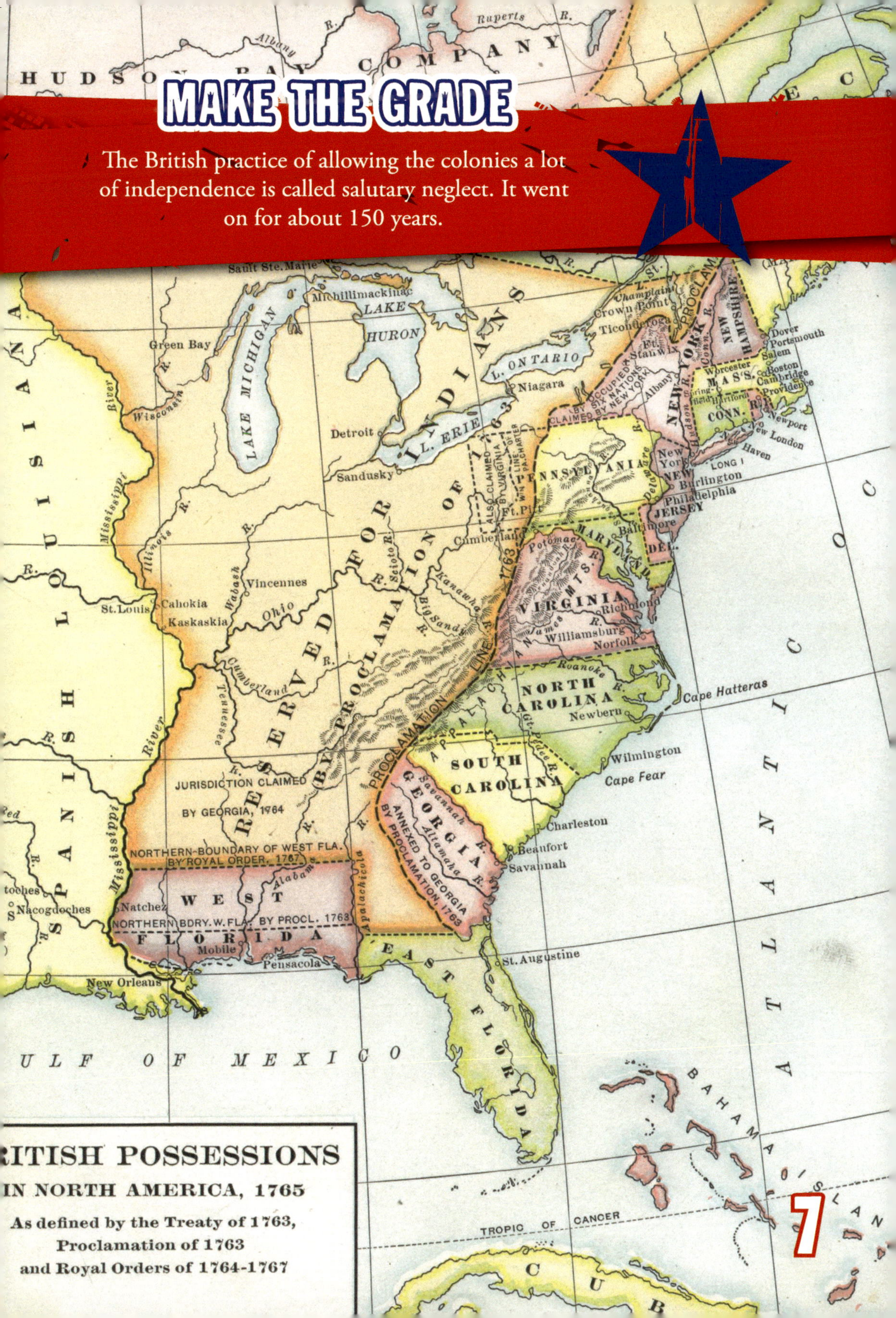

Great Britain tried to raise money by taxing the colonists. In 1764, the Sugar Act taxed sugar. In 1765, the Stamp Act taxed newspapers, cards, and more. Many colonists believed they shouldn't be taxed without having **representatives** in the British government.

newspaper's suggested stamp on taxed goods

MAKE THE GRADE

The Sugar Act and the Stamp Act were **repealed**. But then the Townshend Acts of 1767 taxed glass, paper, and tea.

In 1773, another unpopular law called the Tea Act passed. It gave the British East India Company control of all tea trade in the colonies. Unhappy, a group of colonists dumped tea into Boston Harbor. This is called the Boston Tea Party.

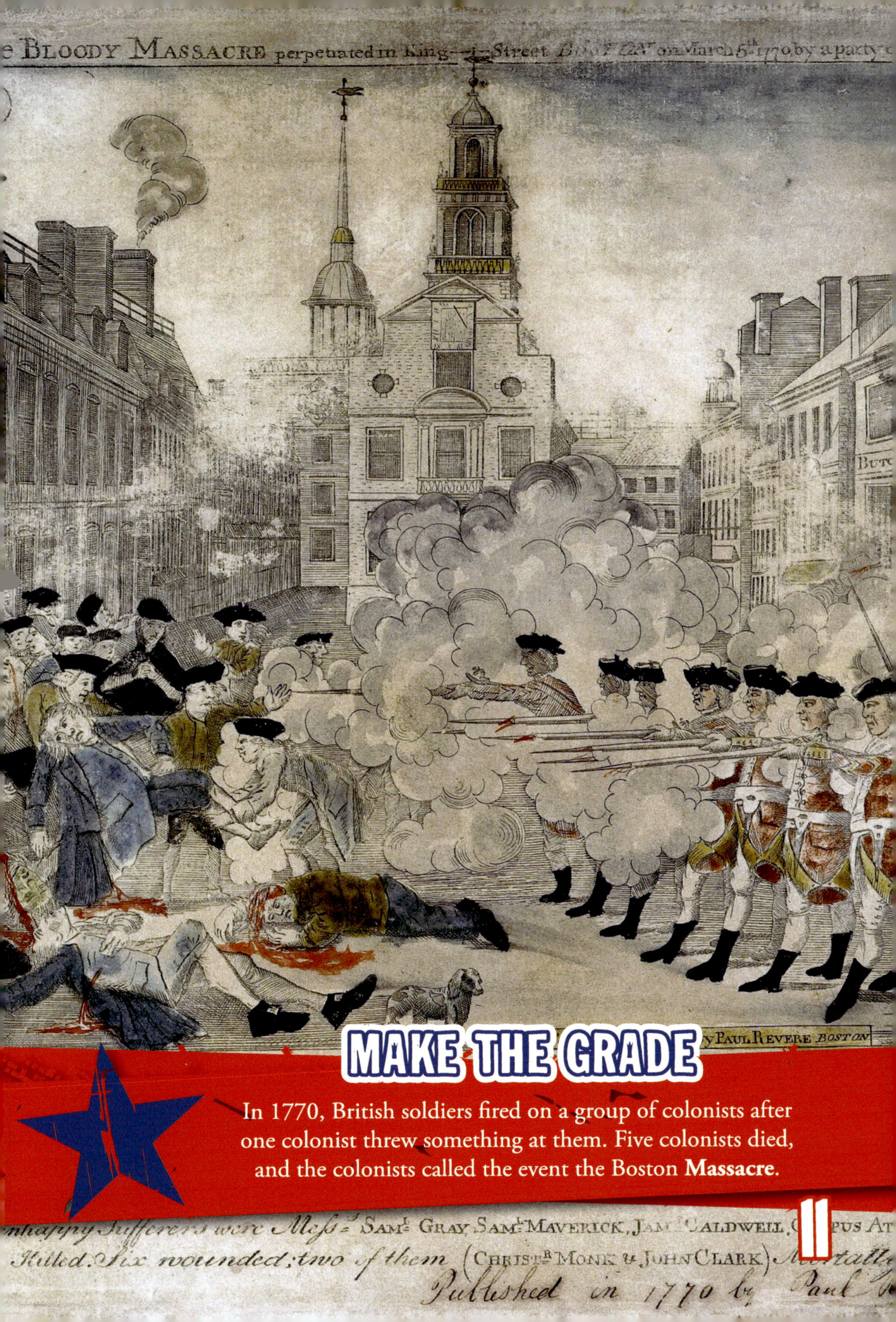

MAKE THE GRADE

In 1770, British soldiers fired on a group of colonists after one colonist threw something at them. Five colonists died, and the colonists called the event the Boston **Massacre**.

After the Boston Tea Party, the British passed the Intolerable Acts in 1774. This group of laws closed Boston Harbor and placed Massachusetts under more British control. This caused 12 of the 13 colonies to meet for the First Continental Congress.

MAKE THE GRADE

The First Continental Congress took place in Philadelphia, Pennsylvania. It called for a boycott of British goods. A boycott is the act of refusing to have dealings with a country in order to force change.

WAR BEGINS

By April 1775, **patriots** in Massachusetts had gathered arms and begun training for war. When the British army arrived in the towns of Lexington and Concord on April 19, **militias** greeted them. No one knows who fired first—but the battles began the war.

MAKE THE GRADE

The British army was trying to take the patriots' arms in Concord. In Lexington, the British were trying to find and capture patriot leaders.

RAISING AN ARMY

Representatives from all 13 colonies met in May 1775 for the Second Continental Congress. The congress formed the Continental army and made George Washington its commander. It also tried to make peace with Great Britain's king, George III. He didn't accept.

MAKE THE GRADE

The Declaration of Independence was written during the Second Continental Congress. It stated that the 13 British colonies would be one, free nation.

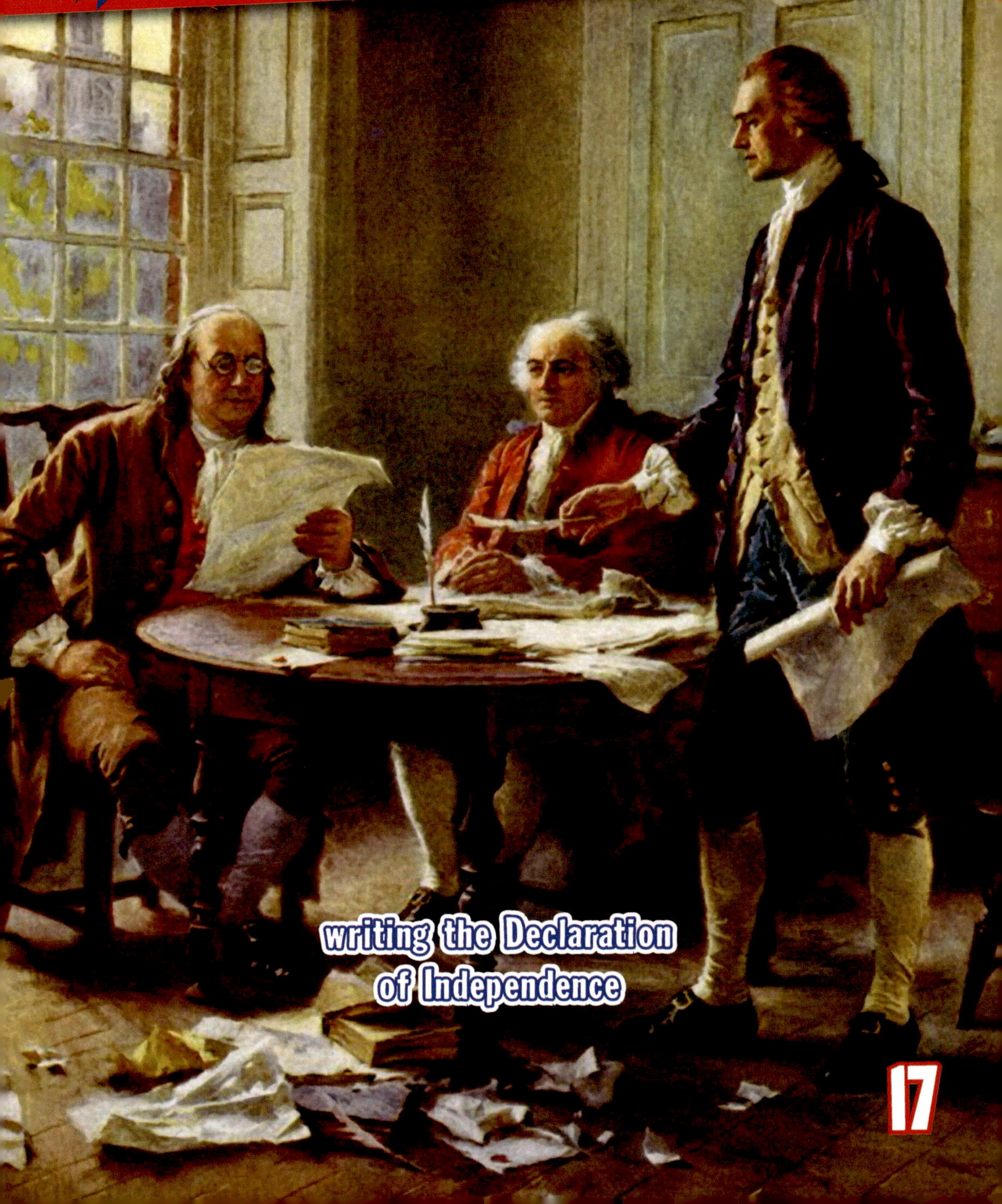

writing the Declaration of Independence

Despite the Declaration of Independence, the war continued. Much of the fighting took place in the North during the first few years. The British forces had a strong navy, which helped them succeed early on.

MAKE THE GRADE

In June 1775, the patriots' forces lost the Battle of Bunker Hill. However, many British soldiers died in the battle, which made the patriots feel they had a chance.

In December 1776, Washington's army got a needed **victory**. The Continental army crossed the Delaware River late at night through winter weather to surprise a British post in Trenton, New Jersey. The victory gave hope to the patriots' cause.

crossing the Delaware

MAKE THE GRADE

The patriots took Fort Ticonderoga in New York in May 1775. It was a stronghold for them until 1777, when British troops forced the Americans out.

THE TURNING POINT

Still, the British continued to succeed in battle. Then, the Continental army won the second Battle of Saratoga in New York in October 1777!

This victory was important. It made other countries believe the patriots' cause wasn't impossible.

MAKE THE GRADE

The Continental army spent the winter of 1777 to 1778 at Valley Forge in Pennsylvania. Food and supplies weren't plentiful, and many men died of illnesses.

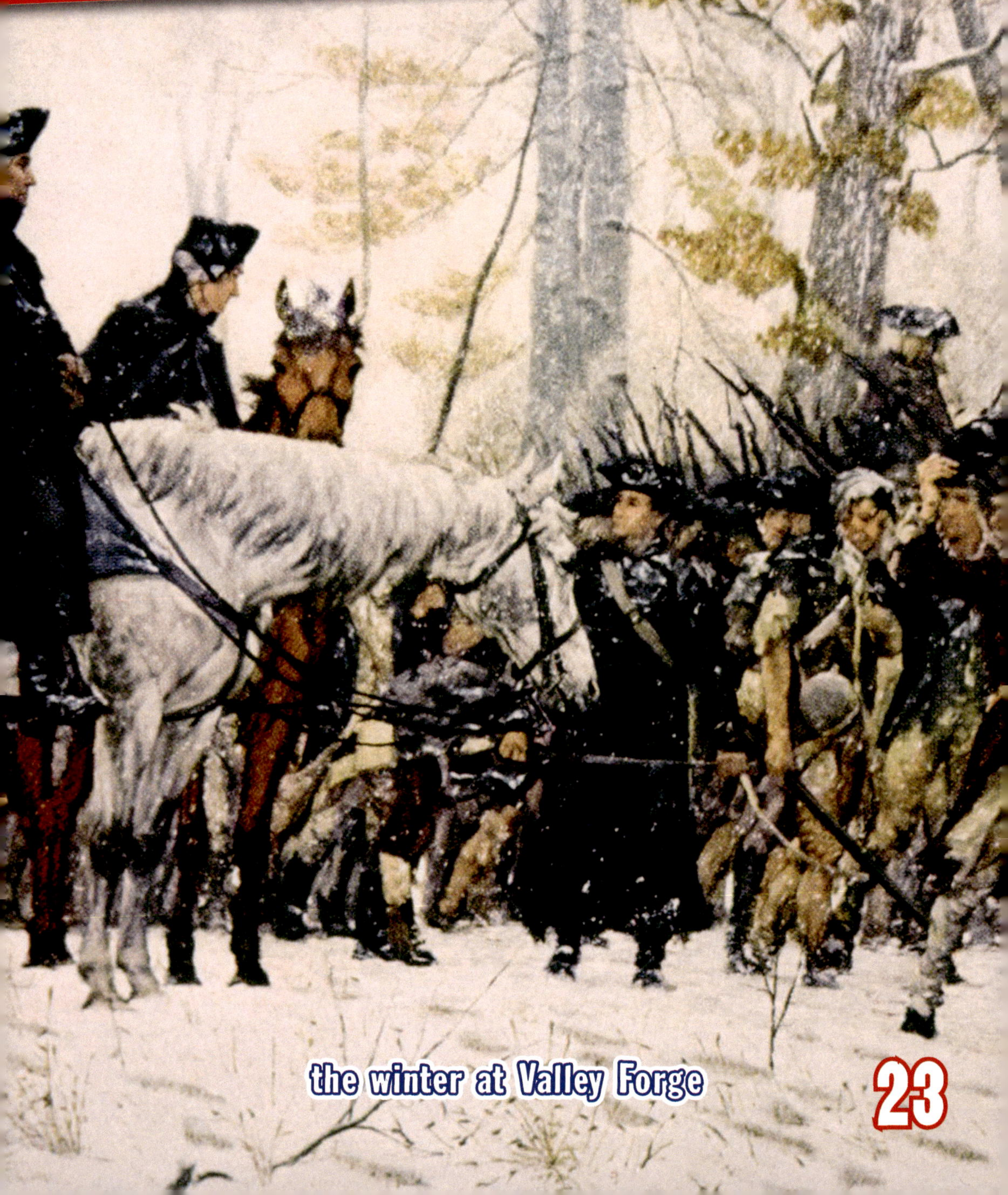

the winter at Valley Forge

A few months after Saratoga, France publicly joined the war on the colonists' side. They had already been quietly giving the Continental army money and arms. In February 1778, the French became the patriots' **ally** and sent thousands of soldiers to fight.

MAKE THE GRADE

The Marquis de Lafayette is the most famous French soldier who fought in the American Revolution. He became a good friend to George Washington.

SURRENDER!

The British took the war to the southern colonies from 1778 to 1781. They won battles, but the Continental army leaders used less traditional **tactics** and began to beat them. With French help, the Continental army forced the British to **surrender** at Yorktown, Virginia.

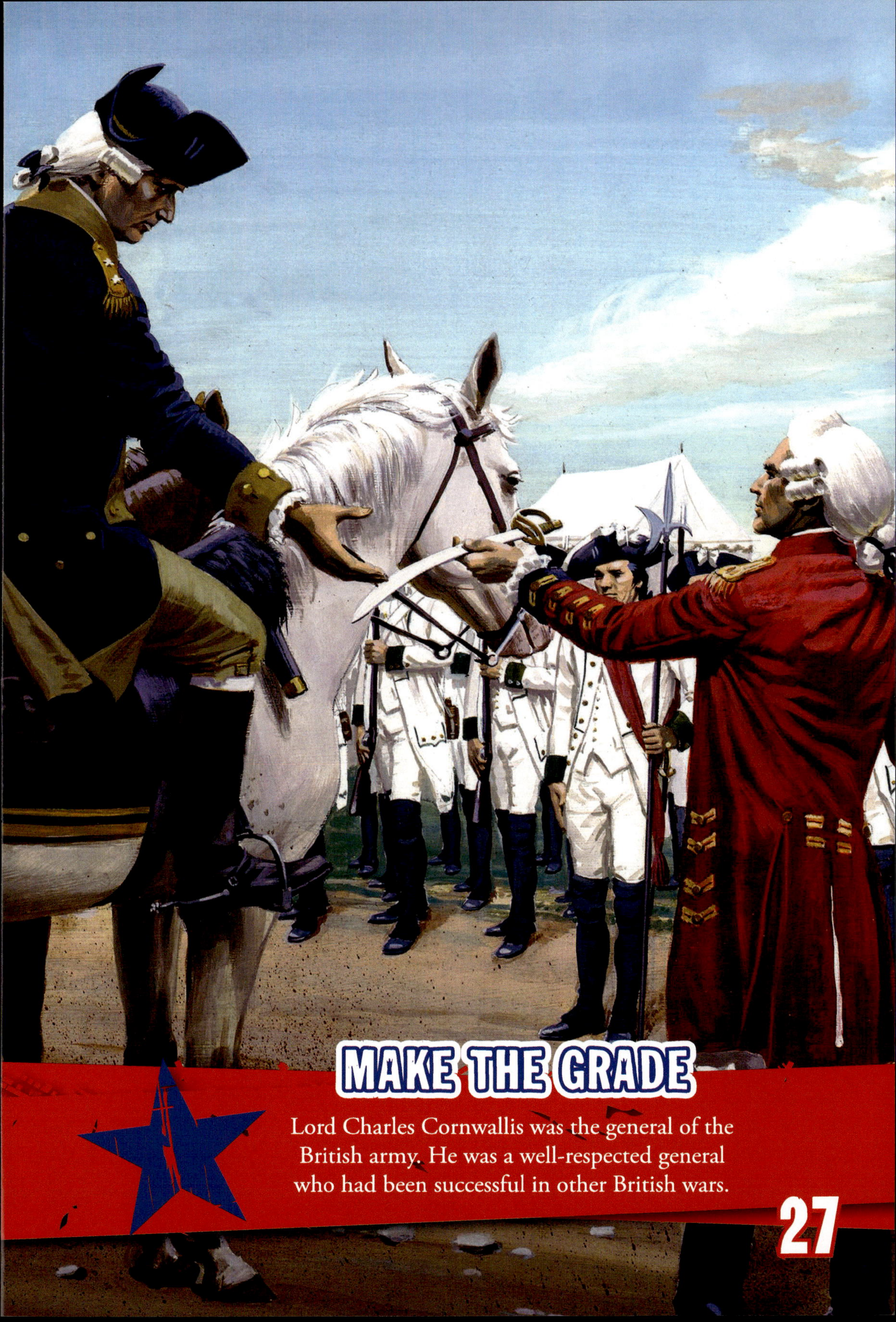

MAKE THE GRADE

Lord Charles Cornwallis was the general of the British army. He was a well-respected general who had been successful in other British wars.

THE TREATY OF PARIS

In 1783, the 13 colonies and the British signed the **Treaty of Paris**. It ended the war and said that Great Britain recognized the 13 colonies as an independent nation. Finally, the new United States set to work creating its own government.

MAKE THE GRADE

The treaty made the borders of the new United States the Atlantic Ocean to the east and the Mississippi River to the west.

TIMELINE OF THE AMERICAN REVOLUTION

September 1774
The First Continental Congress begins.

April 19, 1775
The Battles of Lexington and Concord are the first of the war.

May 1775
The Second Continental Congress begins.

June 17, 1775
The patriots lose the Battle of Bunker Hill.

July 4, 1776
The Declaration of Independence is passed by the congress.

October 7, 1777
The Continental army wins the second Battle of Saratoga.

February 6, 1778
France joins the war on the colonists' side.

October 19, 1781
The British surrender at Yorktown.

September 3, 1783
The Treaty of Paris is signed.

GLOSSARY

ally: one of two or more people or groups who work together

colony: a piece of land under the control of another country

massacre: the killing of a large number of people, especially when they cannot guard themselves

militia: a group of citizens who organize like soldiers in order to keep themselves safe

patriot: a person who loves their country

repeal: to do away with

representative: one who stands for a group of people

surrender: to give up

tactic: a way of accomplishing a military aim

treaty: an agreement between countries

victory: a win over an enemy

FOR MORE INFORMATION

Books

Lanser, Amanda. *The American Revolution by the Numbers.* North Mankato, MN: Capstone Press, 2016.

Marciniak, Kristin. *The Revolutionary War: Why They Fought.* North Mankato, MN: Compass Point Books, 2016.

Websites

American Revolution: Timeline

ducksters.com/history/revolutionarywartimeline.php

Review many events leading up to the American Revolution as well as main events of the war.

Publisher's note to educators and parents: Our editors have carefully reviewed these websites to ensure that they are suitable for students. Many websites change frequently, however, and we cannot guarantee that a site's future contents will continue to meet our high standards of quality and educational value. Be advised that students should be closely supervised whenever they access the Internet.

INDEX